CELLO SIGHT-READING, BOOK 1

by DOREEN SMITH

GRADE 1

© Oxford University Press 1978 and 1992

OXFORD UNIVERSITY PRESS, MUSIC DEPARTMENT, GREAT CLARENDON STREET, OXFORD OX2 6DP

Photocopying this copyright material is ILLEGAL.

Smoothly
11
p
Steadily
pizzicato (plucked)
12
mf
March time
13
mf
cresc.
At a moderate pace
14
mf
smoothly
cresc.
Gracefully
15
mp
Lively
16
mf
p
f
pizz.
Lively
17
f
Fairly quickly
18
mf

Doreen Smith

Cello Sight-Reading

Book 1

NOTE

These graded sight-reading pieces for the cello are designed to provide practice material at all stages. Book 1 begins with the first position and covers the usual examination expectations for the earlier grades. More advanced players will find exercises requiring use of the higher registers, tenor and treble clefs, and the need for more technical expertise in book 2.

Fingering and bowing

There are as many fingerings and bowings as there are players. Those marked here are simply one way of performing a piece; they are by no means obligatory. The aim is to give as musical an impression as possible after a brief study of the piece, and to enjoy exploring the instrument.

To the cellist — what to do before you play

Look at:

- The **foreign words** which will suggest the speed, mood, and style.
- The **key signature**: work out your finger patterns on each string.
- The **time signature**: are you going to count in beats, or would it be more helpful to subdivide each beat?
- **Changes** of clef, key signature, or time signature (in higher grades).
- **Unusual** time patterns, accidentals, rests, staccato notes, slurs, and dynamics.
- The **speed**: decide on the speed and count at least one bar before you begin. Count aloud throughout.

Keep going, and try to give an overall impression of the music.

Doreen Smith, 1992

Quite slowly
19
p
Gracefully
20
mp
f

GRADE 2

Grazioso (gracefully)
1
p

Andante (at a walking pace)
2
mf

Alla marcia (like a march)
3
mf

Allegretto (fairly lively)
4
mf
f

Moderato (at a moderate pace)
5
mf

Allegretto
6
mf

Moderato
7
mf
Andante
8
mf
Adagio (at a leisurely speed)
9
f
Alla gavotta
10
mf
f
Allegro (lively)
11
f marcato (marked)
Waltz time
12
p
Allegro
13
f
p

Allegro
14
f
Moderato
pizz.
15
mf
Adagio
16
mp
cresc.
Allegro
17
mf
mp
cresc.
rit.
f
Giocoso (playfully)
18
mf
f
Andante
19
mp
cresc.
dim.

Lento (slowly)
20
mp
cresc.
dim. e rit.

GRADE 3

Andante
1
mf
p
cresc.
f
dim.

Allegretto
2
mp
cresc.
dim. e rit.

Allegretto
3
mf

Andante
4
mf
mp
cresc.

Moderato
5
mf
mp
cresc.
Moderato
6
mf
f
Waltz
7
mp
mf
dim.
pizz.
Allegro
8
f
Moderato
9
mf
mp
f
Allegro
10
mf
dolce

Allegro
11
mf
p
cresc.
Allegretto grazioso
12
mp cantabile
Allegro moderato
13
f
p
poco rall.
Andante espressivo
14
mf
dim. e rall.
Moderato
15
mf
p
cresc.
1
2
cresc.

Allegretto cantabile
16
mf
poco rall.
Scherzando
17
f
Moderato
18
mf legato
Largo
19
mf
Giocoso
20
mf
pizz.

GRADE 4

Allegretto
1
mf
cresc.

Allegretto
2
mp
mp
dim. e rit.

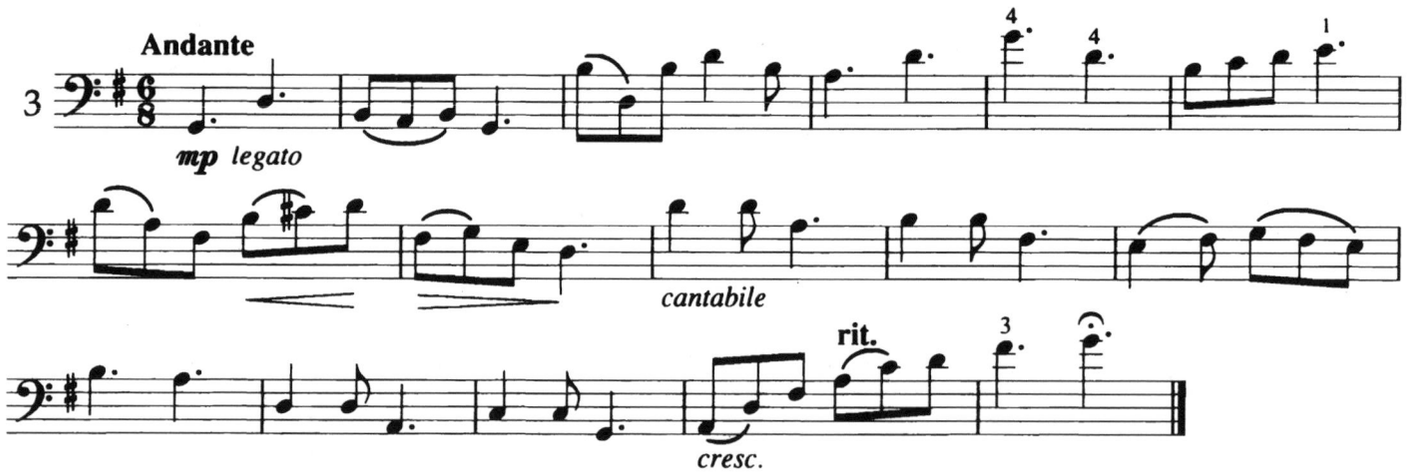
Andante
3
mp legato
cantabile
rit.
cresc.

Andante
4
mf
p
mp

Grazioso
5
mf
cresc.
Allegretto
6
mp
dim.
Andante
7
mp cantabile
pizz.
Moderato
8
mf
pizz.
arco
mf
cresc.
rit.

Moderato
9
mf
cresc.

Allegretto
10
mf

Lento
11
mp espressivo
cresc.
dim. e poco rit.

Allegretto grazioso
12
mp
cresc.
dim. e rall.

Allegro
pizz.
13
mf
p
cresc.
Alla marcia
14
f non legato
mf legato
mp
cresc.
Andantino
15
mf
mp
p
cresc.
Valse
16
p
cresc.
dim. e poco rall.

Allegro moderato
17
f
dolce
pizz.
Giocoso
18
mf sempre staccato
meno f
p
cresc.
Doloroso
19
mp sostenuto
rall. e dim.
Burlesque
20
mf staccato
cresc.
f

GRADE 5

Doloroso
1
mp cantabile
rit.
Allegretto
2
mf
dim.
Vivace
3
mf
cresc.
f
Allegro
4
mf
dim.
cresc.
rit.

Andante
5
mp cantabile
cresc.
dim.
Alla marcia
6
f
mf
cresc.
Moderato
7
mf
cresc.
Andante
8
p legato
dolce
rit.

Vivace
9
mf
p
rit.
Allegretto grazioso
10
mp
cresc.
dim. e rit.
Allegro
11
mf
cresc.
dim. e poco rit.
Largo sostenuto
12
mf
p
poco cresc.
poco rall. e dim.

Allegro marcato
13
f
pizz.
p
cresc.
arco
mp
cresc.
Adagio cantabile
14
mp
p
cresc.
poco dim.
poco rit.
Andante espressivo
15
mp
cresc. poco a poco
poco dim. e rit.
Allegretto
16
mf
p cresc.

17
Vivace
mf non legato
rit.
a tempo
18
Teneramente
p
19
Lento cantabile
p
cresc.
poco rit.
a tempo
più f
20
Larghetto
p
meno mosso
a tempo
mp